AF338260

To Be Held by the Light

To Be Held by the Light

A Lenten Journey

Ariana D. Den Bleyker

RESOURCE *Publications* · Eugene, Oregon

For Jim & Phyllis O'Connell

Contents

Acknowledgments

First and foremost, I would like to praise and thank God the Almighty who has granted the countless blessings, knowledge, and opportunity that enabled me to share these words.

Special thanks to the editors of the following journals in which the following poems first appeared, some in varying forms: *Agape Review*: "Ash Wednesday," "Gone Fishing," "This Is the Time of Loaves & Fish," "My Redeemer in the Wilderness," and "What's Broken Leaves an Entrance for Light"; *As Surely As the Sun Lit*: "On the Water"; *The Clayjar Review*: "The Sap Flows Richly," "The River, Twice," and "Psalm 23 (Revisited)"; *Solid Food Press*: "Born of Water & Spirit"; and *Soul-Lit Review*: "Trust in God."

Many thanks to the following pastors whose sermons during The Reformed Churches of the Wallkill Valley 2023 Lenten Worship Series (The I AM Statements of Jesus Christ) provided great inspiration for many of the poems in this collection: James O'Connell of The First Reformed Church of Walden, NY; Stan Seagren of The Wallkill Reformed Church; Gary Sissel of The Gardiner Reformed Church; David Myers of The New Hurley Reformed Church, Cathy Bruce of The Reformed Church of Shawangunk, and Howie Dalton, Pastor Emeritus, The Wallkill Reformed Church.

Much gratitude and love to James O'Connell whose daily devotions throughout Lent inspired many of these poems and whose love and guidance have spiritually nourished me for nearly twenty years.

To Phyllis O'Connell whose friendship has blessed me with kindness, support, love, and guidance, and taught me what it means to be a true child of Christ for so, so many years.

Finally, to my church family, for making every day feel like Sunday in my heart.

Ash Wednesday,

in the gray weight of its hours extends within the quiet a grittiness—ashes made from last year's palm branches forming a rough & imperfect symbol upon our foreheads. Let me receive this cross of ash upon my brow until the forests of my body burn & I make late repentance of loss while the trees of God clap their hands, the thick smoke soot of palm deepening the peace of a hand extended within the quiet. *You are dust and to dust you shall return*—a beginning & a consummation for all the days I've felt like dust, like dirt, scattered or swept away by the smallest breath. *Cover me with ashes, bring me to my knees, so that in my weakness I see Your strength, the reflection of Your eyes in my brokenness.* Scorched & marked, I've made it through the burning, asked for blessing in the shame & sorrow, the oily smear of ash bearing my sin, my need for grace echoing how well I know it. I want to gather the ash from my face & raise my hands—an offering, an apology. *Remember you are dust.* & so I am. & so I lift my head to meet those words, pardoned, standing in their forgiveness, in the grace of being named. & in my frailty, I am known.

I Will Eat

John 6:48

I've searched the world but it hasn't filled me, & starving in my abundance, I am broken, hungry, & incomplete. I've spilled myself onto the floor of this sanctuary, have grown here as God commands, swelling dark red against the pregnant sea, confessing sin until I've drawn nearer to Christ calling to me until I take the bread & eat & eat of it—this bread hunger in a distended belly's curve, starvation when even the sunrise feels uncertain & everything tastes of bitterness in the wilderness. When darkness clothes my dreams & I tread life waiting for the sea to subside, my repentance now a reflex, a sleepless place where I break Him open & eat again, taste wine so supple I can dip half my fingers in & pull out beautiful fish, sing psalms so sweetly I begin to cry, hold up my hands, palms up, capturing Heaven in both manna & leaven, a body made for everything but itself—in Eucharist, wafer thin, provision like dew every morning feeding me one moment at a time in this space where my emptiness cries out as I boil & bake what is given to me, tasting the sweetness of it all, both held & raised up among a pillar of cloud, weighed down with the rain, & then, snow.

On the Water

Matthew 14:22–36

& I alone, surrounded by hills in the darkness, struggle against the water, boat pitching at 3 a.m. in the midnight blue, & when the winds pick up & the dark water rises, *Fear not* becoming the most spoken imperative but doubt comfort in this wild, untamed life, my basic biology betrays me: racing heart, sweat, breathlessness, a brokenness devoid of God—me, over my head in this world, terrified in the turbulence, the danger despite Christ perpetually moving toward me. & for a moment, I step out in faith, dazzled out of doubt for a beautiful, flickering instant until I stumble into the darkness, until I pull my eyes from Him & drown in all the what-ifs leaving me flailing again & again & again. But when he meets me, catches me, & I am left shivering in perfect stillness, mine is the boat He climbs into. & I will stare into His eyes, a little bit of Peter inside me, & I will walk on water.

This Is the Time of Loaves & Fish

Matthew 13:14–21

People are hungry, & one good word is bread for a thousand against the 5,000 swallowing remnants of a miracle into hungry bellies called out into hope, for silence cannot nourish the body because I am hungry & thirsty & come to the table to leaven my life, to discover, to trust when it doesn't make sense. *Lord, I believe, help my unbelief.* Let's put all our chips into the middle of the table, expose the lack in our hands. The world is hungry; feed a sea of people with small loaves & fish—whatever is in Your hand. Your tent is light enough to spring up around You yet heavy enough to darken the stars. & this world is a gift, these bodies the same, but life incomplete—*They must be hungry.* Emmanuel, God with us, You hunger too—feed us Your very self—& we'll take what we need & pass it on, the miracle in the sharing, manna from Heaven, provision for the hungry receiving Eucharist directly from the hands of Christ, a boy's small lunch broken & shared as the bounty of Heaven moved not only by beauty of holiness but also by the holiness of beauty.

Miracles, an Act of Love

John 2:1–11

Wine, that joy, the blood of the grape run out, much richer than happiness in the sight of God's intention to bring together creation, or revelation, a blessing embracing ritual for the encouragement of fruit as gift spoken out of the sky, an ultimate act of love in a moment when Heaven is opened, when transformation bursts into the world, intersections of telling & listening, of making use of water, six stone jars of salvation quenching thirst, a temporal cleansing of bodies from dirt, from sin, made forever in baptism in the blood of Christ, the true vine, a covenant of love, an invitation, redemption raised in the east in glasses where any angled light would congregate endlessly under the weight of His words, true joy, eternal & finished.

God Waits in Hope

Luke 15:3–7

In days of song, in a world of noise, in spaces of challenge, in paths of peace & in sanctuaries of silence, everything is still in this pasture, the water restful & right. I stand in the mountains, live where a church rests on a hill, & I shall not ask for the help of dying trees whose fruit, though ripe, would leave me with less or perhaps more than I can bear. The shepherd sings to me an old folk song, & I am not worthy, though I should not want in this valley of darkness. What joy is raised in this pasture of thirsty hearts, & the 99 say *don't stray into the fog in the hills.* But I must lay down my life to take it up again. Find me quiet now in my wandering, let me hear your song of grief. Seek me & I shall follow, be brought back into the flock, into the fold again. The afternoon is hot. Wrap me around your shoulders, bear my cross, Lamb of God, who pays the cost of bringing me home, let me hear your song as you celebrate my forgiveness, & we, all the one, drink deep while we can & be thankful for our thirst.

What's Broken Leaves an Entrance for Light

John 8:12

In the small spaces of knowing, I was there lying broken when God smiled & the light broke. & when he took it into His hands & flung it against the maw of darkness, its vibrations shifted through me, threads of light from a waking sun—the language of God, of source, where we root & nourish, giving us body, an ancestral light we feel from the inside when even the deficit of light brings more light—light chasing light—like igniting a match & swallowing the flame, the taut, warm light allowing us to glow a distant orange in our histories, a bright star in the east burning echoes in our throats, fire in our chests, our bodies eternal burning bushes, fragile bundles, brutal & beautiful, woven together of joy & sorrow, every one of us a fire, relics of holy flame, with God giving back the discomfort of hope in all the brightness we carry. & in the breathing of these moments, we take off our shoes & learn a name that's no name: I Am what I Am, the irrevocable & benevolent light shining through us & in each heart a Bethlehem. I understand this light to be my home.

My Redeemer in the Wilderness

Luke 4:1–13

That He might be tempted, that in Him Adam & Eve, Job, Israel's golden calf, & ourselves, might walk this dark yet strangely tempting valley to dwell in the house of the Lord forever, a house darkened by no shadow of temptation, no lust, no ambition, no avarice. That I was hungry, tongue scorched white, turned inside myself against the wilderness, having known times of suffering, the weeping tarries of night, & hard fought for morning's joy. The battle for faith ugly, the refining fire excruciating. There is no strength in myself deepened by suffering, union with God, weakness & vulnerability. & it's true that I found Him, shriveled with hunger, shivering in the desert, skeletal, emaciated, nothing to warm His bones once the bright sun set. & we spent hours discussing God at the mouth of His cave. I heard the dull, hollow echo of silence, a strange communion between us, waves taking shape in His features. I saw Him delving deep into death, the last dance delayed. He knows the way there, knows the front door to the silent garden, begs to take us there to our shadowy oasis in a wave of drought, like looking into a mirror at Adam or Job, lonely in their grief & isolation, led into temptation to crown all temptations. That I watched Him sit at God's table, full of fear for my own fragility & wondered how He dared own so much of Himself, openly, wanting to dare to believe some things in this world must be far too lovely to ever be broken— my body dust & bone, criminal in my living as seemingly innocent as rain. That I can take Him as my companion in suffering—eat & sleep beside him, walk behind Him blindfolded, our wounds shared, learning how not to abandon the body's weight & how to make the body expand, to keep becoming, until even the danger could not swallow me, to watch what falls from the sky in those moments we know brokenness to be true, to have a taste of Heaven & quench the need of being human, to believe in light radiating, penetrating my body that is neither ether nor the Word incarnate. That I am letting go to God's power made perfect in my weakness.

Pilgrimage

Psalm 121

i.

God is a mountain inside me, standing still where the breezes stir;
He is rooted, forging channels through my body, keeping me alive
& faithful. Distant from the hope of myself, he saves me daily. & I,
with my hungry mouth, lift my jagged arms to pray, the coolness of
untainted air deep in my lungs, the mountain only growing steeper
so that I may dig deeper, holding my breath, ascending inside the
one hand that raises me. My feet carry my weight, vulnerable to the
giving & taking of the day, the cold & shadows of the night. God
keeps me, & I am alive in hope as He climbs beside me, battered by
the sun & taken by the darkness.

ii.

I toss my faith like a stone into the air & it touches something blue
like that time I climbed a mountain in the middle of a storm just
to smell the rain & spent the afternoon feeling less alone knowing
that storms crawl across the skies to grow things. & I am cured
by God alone, living by a faith that looks a lot like a mountain
catching the sunset & breaking the light into a thousand glittering
suns. I want to be the happiness closer to God, to be nearer to the
sky, the smell of lavender journeying with me to hidden heights,
the taste of feasts remaining, the mountain & the bells of the flock
reminding me where I lay my hope, my heart climbing still, stark
against the sky. Here, I am home.

Gone Fishing

Matthew 4:19

It's almost as if I can smell the air of Galilee, hear waves crashing, the thin, clear of water no map can name, hidden places. I love the way I find them, the way I follow no channel, just sound tangled in the shore to where slow water opens a hole to cast a net into & lift from the well bright shadows of Heaven fish held in my hand, the air around me alive, the water cooler & clearer, the sun brighter, the sky bluer, the fishermen surrounding me casting their nets methodically, cheerfully.

*

In the waveless sea, deep blue under deep blue, the fisherman drifts by in His tiny vessel. Above Him the cloud-capped hills, & He flicks his wrist, throws a net across continents. I can hear it swish, slice clouds, going wherever there's water, gathering the surge of body & fin, a miracle—the submerged shaft of sun split like spun glass swiftly moving into the crevices, in & out, illuminates the turquoise sea of my body, grabbing at my soul like a lion in a cage until I long for the smell of fish.

*

& the fisherman says, *Follow me.* & He smiles until I shed my scales for Him. & with a song on my lips, I too become a fisherman, raising my net, casting my soul, reeling in love, joy, peace, patience, goodness, kindness, faithfulness, gentleness, self-control, the fruits of the spirit; my cast not a question of strength so much as a relinquishing, that the net's release is an extension from the wrist to the heart. & I'll keep casting my net, & when it does not come back empty, I'll step again into that small boat that carried me out & watch the bank recede—facing Heaven, trying again & again to find that perfect cast, gathering up the braids to find the fish writhing in my hands.

Born of Water & Spirit

John 3:1–6

& I ached in that moment, longing for restoration, my spirit heavy with the weight of invisible fruit—the soul of myself ripe. & I felt the seed of it sending its roots, silently, through my stillness. How to describe that moment when we become, this awakening? I calculated the distance between womb & Heaven, dreaming a dream for God to show me what I was & who I'd become, the breath my chest carrying promise. I was awake, silver water spilling, less than arms-length in the patient opening of one long-awaited flower, the quiet mechanics of one perfectly-crafted key turning the lock of my body as I crowned through blood & water, slowly, slowly—right shoulder reaching out until I felt my sharp edges soften from the touch of God. This new life, this plucked silence, a teardrop—the Spirit sweeping over the face of the waters, knitting me together once more, wind-like, dove-like, holding me as I became & Christ awakened in my body from above through God's cupped hands.

When There Are Storms

Psalm 91

God: how I curl beneath You, heart against Your chest, as if testing the strength of its walls, my rib cage splayed, knees felled away from each other, Your refuge a home where I unfold myself, retreat into You, protected, vulnerable & raw. With Your outstretched arms unfurled, You bring structure to my chaos, steadiness to uncertainty, shelter inside the temple of Your bones, comfort in Your light, the way Your body blankets mine. Lord, let me climb into You again & again. There I will dwell, rest in the stillness, inside an umbrella of feathers surrounding me like faith returning when everything else is gone.

The Shepherd Holds Watch

John 10:1–10

There's a pasture of sin between us, between me & who I was meant to be, but You have led me out of brown & barren fields & into the fold, & I bow down my head. An angel's wing arcs up in the sky, erecting a steeple that points upward as faith goes. Part of who I was is scattered behind from which I've returned to you & into the pasture. I see the door, the sunlight & know the wall—the sheepfold echoing your song. & I feel the pulse of a new day in the end of this day. & I am already at the door (not the one broken down by thieves, not the one You've built with Your own hands, but the one You've become—load-bearing, gently hinged—to bridge the gap in the wall, to nestle us inside the fold), digging the earth with my feet to enter the fold. & walking through the door is like walking into a warm house. I'm full, more full, more beautiful as I grow outside my body & my comfort flourishes like the wild grass I graze in the heat of the summer. You've laid Your body down across the threshold—Your body the door that opens my home—& You call my name & I lay down to dwell with You.

Scattering the Word

Matthew 13:1–23

He strides across the freshly plowed field scattering seeds from His sack, the field stretching like a dark sea to the horizon, bleeding into the rising sun. The earth is ripe & soft & awaiting this moment, longing for this seed, eager for renewal, hungry, not caring if it's rose or weed, strong or sturdy, or spindly & sprawling, jubilant for the aroma of tender shoots, lilacs & blossoms, a time for new beginnings—the thrown seeds permeating broken ground, the silhouetted sower scattering seeds to feed man, stave his hunger—some finding stone, thorns, & hard earth—scorched, chocked, picked clean; others taken by the wind, fed by the voice of gentle rain, rooted, broken open, sewn where there is promise. Here is the rich soil. Here is God's plenty.

Our Good Inheritance

Psalms 16

There is joy in darkness—bright orange rising in the one patch of new grass gleaming with spring, catching all of the early sun. I sit quietly, unrestrained in the dark, hope immovable & know Your love is not a Band Aid or duct tape; Your love is a seatbelt, a map, a life jacket—

or—

life jackets strung together like colorful paper lanterns wrapped around our bodies floating above the darkness, a place where we learn to love water & sun angles just so, the sun connecting us to the water & new world where we lie on our backs & watch the clouds changing, knowing we'll never drown in salty water, that without the jackets we'll learn to swim in Your deep depths. & as You empty the heavy stones of darkness from our pockets, allowing us to catch our breaths, feel the sun shining on our faces, we'll have faith in your absence, & we'll shake off the dust of our dying moments to come home blessed, & that in that home we'll be saved.

This Is My Origin Story

Matthew 13:31–32

Empty hands are all I have. The nothing in the valley of my palm is all You need to place the mustard seed—my body soil with room for roots. Take & tend my seed; it is there, deep in my young heart bearing fruits of faith, sharing my belief You love me. Fill me, fill me with all the living water to grow a mighty mustard bush bearing more fruits, bringing shelter, roots sprawling inside my bones. I harvest the power of faith from my hands, the power to move mountains placed inside my palm that has grown from seed to bushes to trees where the birds gather—acres of yellow born from the west wind bringing the rain, the south winds thunder—seeds scattering, inhaled, breaking on the tongue, the miracle of seed within me, one infinite grain divided like loaves & fishes, as if from the great concourse of birds at home there, wings among yellow flowers, a body grown & grown & grown into a landscape, a belly full of seed sprawling, how it unfurls for acres & acres, a body, a heart, finding home in faith, a woman waiting to be sown.

Beauty in Broken Things

2 Corinthians 12

Scattered, I fell among the thorns, still hungry to grow, & so I grew with them, made a tall tree of my arms, raising my palms to the sky to take in the rain, the little light filtering through the cracks in the sky while the thorns fattened all around me until one broke my flesh, digging deep in between my ribs. & it grew, year after year, remaining under the folds of my skin until one day, with face tilted up, a new seed fell in my open mouth, rainfall awakening it on the stub of my tongue, & it took root, brought forth shoots in the readiness of my soul, & all at once I knew the vulnerabilities of my thorn, knew to make whole His absence; our bodies yoked, squatting deep with the weight of my thorn, thighs strained, heels digging into fertile soil, taking new root, gorging on strength. We shouldered the weight, braced for bad weather, our faces glowing brightly, my faith crawling up from inside the red stretches of my throat, sounding almost like an echo so important there could be no silence in the gap between what was & is, releasing with it joy, what was above me within me, my thorn protection, strength in humility, humility to accept my brokenness. & with it, I pictured Christ, brow against thorn, His grace within is hollow, His crown twined with *every* thorn. & just as broken clouds give rain, broken grain bread, broken bread life, He offers His strength perfect in our weakness.

The Water We Were Meant to Drink

John 4:1–26

I lie here, barren land in my mouth, tongue aching, throat hot
for water, & I speak to You, a faint prayer cast from parched lips
longing for living waters, fresh rain leading me to You. My burning
body is a well dug deep down to the heart of the earth where a
spring of hope, silver water waits for me to fill my cup. & when
the Spirit comes in & rolls through the cool dampness of the well,
blows hard across the earth & climbs the waves of my heart, rises
& bends until I hear my heart boom inside Yours, I am no longer
dry but thankful for my continued thirst.

Stepping Over the Threshold

John 14:1–14

I woke this morning in the gold light turning this way & that, thinking for a moment of how the sun spoke, telling of how still the morning grows, how slow morning comes so the birds may lend their church to me, a sanctuary sown in the air, realized in the body ushering windows, growing rafters, planting seeds— blessings sown upon me daily, so endless these gifts, like manna in the morning. & this morning God walked through this sanctuary setting the clocks for spring. I stood at the window long enough to hear His word & I leaned across the day & miles of sea to become the broken seed in a lamplit house filled with fertile soil. & I tilled the floors & rooms of my Father's house, & I didn't count the hours as I turned the dirt over & under for nothing but love—mine for him & His love for me waiting in a bigger, brighter room of the house. & I heard the Son as though He tilled beside me, a Son whose name I knew to say softly. & when He crossed the threshold & laid down beside me in the room of my arrival, He knew I called Him, & He answered. He knew my frailty, that I'll soon be ashes, my life an ember or a mustard bush in a field, His field, wind passing over—the Spirit claiming me for Him & how much this house is my house, my body the home of God where He & I dwell, a little house whose humble roof protects me & this cot I lie on with strong beams & floors, quiet candlelight filling the room, & all the angels of Heaven ascending through the first roof of light the sun has made. This, the bright home in which I live, where I ask my friends to come, where I want to love all the things it has taken me so long to learn to love. This is the temple of my belonging, & I will dwell in the house of the Lord my whole life long.

My Shepherd Calls

John 10:1–6

& I see the voice shine with fullness, hear the voice that spoke in the beginning, on the morning of that first day when light burst out of the darkness, & I drag my fingers across the still waters, hold my arms out into the winds to feel this—this caressing, this giving & taking of space. I hear His voice in clear skies, cloudy days, dark nights, listen to the silence & its speaking in languages only I know—I can hear His words, His voice clearly by my side bouncing off my own. He calls to me in earthquakes & weather, leans down into my thankfulness, tickles my ears with truth. & I grow in it, feed on it, know it. When the evening comes, I will follow. I will enter the fold after He has called me home, break bread, listen to the calmness of those still waters in the quiet of dawn, the morning that never fades.

The Sap Flows Richly

John 15

I was alone, made of rain & soil, twists in vine, to grow, to burrow roots, & draw from silt, truth & grace, & You bent toward me in a mile-wide sky with a soothing voice, hovered over the stacked vine, the pliant, supple stalks. The heavy air leaned on me. You docked the dead, the damaged, & diseased. You clipped & cropped, making the kindest cuts, as you pruned me under the luminous moon of early evening, the smell of broken vines & leaves, the discarded sprigs on the ground an offering. I paused in your work—breathed, observed, felt, moved toward holiness where I was grafted into you—this beautiful inheritance—a cluster of grapes of the Promise Land two men carried back to the desert as blessing, proof I can become imperfectly gentle, good as drops of water on turned dirt. & in time when the sky cracks with lightning, my stalks will hold rain again, & all the waiting & uncertainty will pale behind colors of life-bearing fruit, & I will swell & bloom again.

The River, Twice

Luke 3:21–22

God dwells within me. Inside me, water sways like a cradle rocking me, drawn like the tide to the moon, I carry my water & it carries me. Let me float into the heavens, let me unfold, be reborn immersed in the Jordan. There He will comfort me—a sky, air, light—an awakening. *Beloved* coming like a mercy to the ear, like this river to my body. Comes holy. Comes healing. Drenched as I am in my love for Him born anew by grace. I am a sliver of flesh re-entering the womb of light. I am Your *beloved* welcoming this weightlessness. I want to be buried in it; feel the gust of air, palms up reaching for the firmament while the river spills its guts in deep music; I wade out, return with a yearning I cannot name, casting off my sin like it's an old coat. I am a star, a yellow seed turned tree, that fountain in the sun; I am *beloved*. He knows me. There is a great force moving through us, between us, connecting us as we walk into the river mud, the bright sky behind us a sheet of gray light. The mist of morning still clings to the water, & a long slender shape appears, gliding in the distance, & as the shape comes closer, the air clears, wings stretched in flight, gliding low out of the torn heavens, the sun transforms the river. I sink into the muck along the wet banks. Home. See the dove descend, gentle as love, vibrant with the breath of the Spirit moving over the water, its breast beating & pulsing with grace, full of joy. Here the voice of Heaven declaring goodness in His *beloved*. Hear the Word speaking the goodness, a blessing. Attend to the wing, the descending, the voice, the follow by grace to a joyful future. I enter the wilderness but do not begin without blessing, do not leave without traveling the path He had carved out before me, do not go without letting the word *beloved* echo in my journey. Though He cannot promise this blessing will free me from fear, from hunger or thirst, from the scorch of the sun, fall of night, He will be there in rest & in comfort, in the strength behind & in front of me leaning Himself toward my ear, whispering my name—*beloved*, the gates of Heaven thrown wide open to me, the Holy Spirit given to me—who I was erased in the flash of baptism, stillness calling me inward—I am eternally reborn.

Psalm 23 (Revisited)

This comfort beckons, repeating itself from memory, a reverberating peace—solace of stones in thin water, hunched like the spines of sheep, the water whispering a perfect circle drawn by God. I am fearfully & wonderfully made, formed within the flock & guided through pastures & roughly hewn hills where gentle winds glide me along heavenly currents beside the expansive green canopies He folds over me at night. & when I've fallen into the smoothness of the stream, I can feel a rock resonating with my bones—the wind sculpting the rock cupping the water escaping as wind—movement & stillness in the same body. A million exhales rise from within me & travel outward & forward into a grace flooding the ruins of my heart, all the wounded, desolate places searched out, filled with light—restored by His voice until new strength comes & weariness has passed. His path is a supple bolt of cloth, shaken & rolled out, laying itself down in a new way across the hills I climb without knowing what's on the other side. & it is in the valley I grow; full-throated & roaring, I curl around the low woods, climb into the white mist & rock where slanting rays of sun fall, forming a belt of brightness until the shadows become white light & I readjust my steps along the radiant flow. Surrounded & enfolded, a fire breathes in the space between my ribs simply because He is there. I melt into another world, a realm of strength already within me, & I change—I soften with joy, stand there in His path, see my feet in the fold. The sun glistens on the vines that twine & open at the edge of the ravine, & I sing before the ceaseless swell & fall of sunlight on the hills, watch the way brilliance turns on darkness forever.

Something Strong & Beautiful

Psalm 139:1–18

At the moment of my birth, I shone with immeasurable light,
wide-eyed, emerging like the brightest star, Your word spoken
through me, Your language lifting me into place, embraced by vast,
light-laden arcs, a speck of hope only You knew among the farthest
reaches of the night sky; Your eyes saw in the black, perceiving the
fainted glow, a tiny spark from before I knew myself. & there was
stillness tucked deep, circled within the thickness of Your love, a
consciousness slipping into the vast ocean from where I came & I
can barely hold this love in my hands, soaked in undeniable surety.
& I want to save each fracture second of it all. & I know this is
home like the way my breathing ebbs & flows in a quiet grace when
I lay my face against Your chest—or every time I hear Your voice.
& I want to hold on to all of this & be carried to where I want to
go, to where I lay my body inside You & give into your knowing,
a free fall into the Spirit, into everything. Every night I am here in
this quiet darkness, reaching out for You, & You move into me like
water, like moonlight. How strong & beautiful Your love is for me
like new meadows across decimated bones. You build something
lush with the strength of red woods inside me, every bend of a
stream an inlet somewhere, a warm little corner where the currents
churn slow & soft across worn rocks. & I am an inlet You search
out to gather & hold. Yes, I was born of wilderness & wind, born
of narrow roads, hidden where I walked & held Your hand. I was
born in the orange-red sunrise of morning, born of forgiveness,
formed on a slate washed clean into the particles of love that define

me, the common sea of consciousness between us where I always feel you beside me. & I rejoice, sing to the underside of clouds, deep in the valley where You are with me.

29

To Be Held by the Light

John 9:1–23

The strength it took to see, to be & all I want is to be held to You & never let go. I'm heavy with the weight of time, too many times I have been blind before I began to tell everyone that in even those moments, of feeling dark & unrelenting, there could be infinite beauty if I allowed myself to open my eyes, darkness into light, a holiness where the shadows of the pines rise straight & tall & dark against the languishing light of day, fire streaked across the sky & all the peaks beneath illuminate with stillness. & how the orange-red remnants of the sun push through the empty spaces recessed within me, motionless bodies of the conifers solemn as stone. & when dusk comes quiet through the timber & there is no more hiding, just the gentle truth He knows, this forest, climbing wide across the ravines into the mountains hold me, & though it could let me go like the yellowed leaves scattered on the ground like the last glow of the evening sun touching the canopies of trees, You reach across this void & hold my hand & I am pulled back to where I began, like the way it feels each time I lay down in Your arms. I'd like to still my heart where I am suspended in weightless space, a resting space between the deep & sunlight, & I turn my cheek to caress Your firm hands each time You smear mud across my eyes. You are the only one whose arms around me will ever be enough.

The Fruit of Good Action

Mark 11:14; 20–25

I was a fig tree spreading my generous canopy across the spring hillside when You approached me with caution, hoping for just one edible fruit. You reached up into the branches, reached up for the fruit that should hang, a fig whose skin would just begin to bear the flesh of readiness, but there was no such thing—nothing grown softer & fuller, & You cursed my lack of promise. & as the last fat, yellow leaves fell from me, I was bare, a barren womb asleep inside the trunk within fresh dirt, white, clean stones jutting from its base, no fruit, a wasteland, nothing ripe for the taking. I stood withered, a bone-white sepulcher, dead branches clutching the sky against the lush, green background; and yet, though dark with damp decay, a rare beautiful fragile corpse, I still felt Your work within me, felt You making me fruitful & bountiful, creating music in my bones until the branches danced. If you listen very carefully at the precipice of dawn, there where the hills lift the thickened fog into a brightness of sky, there are quiet leaves of hope & the fluttering of my heart reborn. I lay down my body at the temple of the hills, & when I let go, free fall into the wind beneath the cliffs, Your arms are the endless fractals of sky that reach down to grab me, & I can feel them. I am not afraid to disintegrate, to fall to my knees & break, to breathe in the light, to blush, to ripen, hold myself the way fig flesh folds itself into each hour, its skin rubbed from gray to purple. I listen for You, for the fruit, tender & sticky & all I can do is hunger, become the true fig parting the leaves like a sign, slipping into Your outstretched palm when the morning sky opens clear, the leaves gathering sunrise like stained glass windows, & I am filled with happiness so pure it feels like innocence, & I find You flowering inside me.

32

An Axe-Shattered Window

John 14:6

This morning brightens almost unnaturally into a rusting, burnished, purplish-red haze & everything bursts into flame. Prayers cut rivers down my face & pour heavily to the floor, & in gazing up at You, I swirl outside myself—here & not here, fear making a home of my body. There is nothing but hope in being lost in vulnerability, or how Your unfaltering belief in me—all that I am, & was, & could be, shows only *You* know me. Draw me in, hands gentle as the calm outside my window, caress my face, & when You press into me, reach in & yank the last remnants of fear from me. I have called for Your voice & kneeled here, begging to be stripped bare, heart beating wildly, no longer afraid of the violent power of this wild space. & in You, I find myself again. & so, I extend my hands out into the darkness, fingertips aching to find You shifting through the wind as my skin splits at the window's edge, panes dissolved & fear pouring out, bent over, arms clutched across my chest, sobbing, entering a silence where all the suffering hangs heavily suspended in the resonance of flame, & here too, your love carries & lifts. Heal me & forgive my blindness; take my hand & show me *home* & a crisp silence broken only by the crackling of honesty. There's thirst on my tongue, running down my throat, & You are the only way when the heat rests heavy on the skin. When my hurt becomes audible, You comfort me. Come straight for me, hold me up, tear me down until my bones turn outside. There's nothing like the truth, like the way you move inside me. Let me fall into you & know that you're still behind me, in front of me, all around me. I will lean into you before I fall. In your presence I can stand without shaking & fullness is silence & the aching of flight without wings. There is a space between my ribs where you enter, & the tears that cease when you settle in. & the wind feels like freedom, & the fire is beating with some kind of barely audible drum. But, You are a whisper shouting silently in my ear, & I can feel the faint whisper of *this is home* in my bones. So I let your arms wrap around me, feel my skin cascade, my ribs break, & suddenly, from my naked heart, know I am home. I will let you in, breathe. I will throw my head back with my mouth wide open & I will draw you down to the hollows of my bones where you will take in my marrow & carry it from the fear & doubt. This wasteland is dying. Lift the surface & expose the verdant roots within.

The Faithful Cry Out

Psalm 130

There is a darkness, no, a space of emptiness where everything is mist & fog & stretches forever with no beginning or end. & I can see it when I close my eyes & am drowned by the thickness of this dense shroud laying heavy between the broken fragments of my peace. The whales are crying in the trenches of the sea & their songs cannot find me here. Melodies weep through the mantle of the earth; liturgy seeps through the ocean floor & I am pulled to the deep where there are fathoms in Your eyes. Let me sleep beneath the blood moon tides, beneath the starlight glinting off the crashing seas above me. & in this moment, for some reason, I'm cold & thinking of snow—the way it could fall upon my face & deafen my rough voice. But, if I close my eyes for too long, I'll miss the brightness of the morning melt the ice. & though it may cut hard, the warmth of Your mercy will lay my palms out to clutch it. *Reach with me* into the crackling cold & let me feel something so pure I'll want to taste it, the crystals dripping onto my tongue—diamonds floating down from clouds so thick & white, this stabbing pain will be shredded into the kaleidoscope of light of Your eyes. & there is stillness in the endless sleep tucked deep beneath this snow, curled within the thickness of the earth, released out of the depths, a consciousness freed to slip back into that vast ocean, but then there is this cry that falls & cuts hard into my inner backbone & how in one, single moment, I know I can barely hold it all in my hands. The light filtering through the snow is brighter than before, yet at my back, the shadow still creeps into me. I am not an effigy of my sorrow but an elegy for the storm. See how the darkest water parts along the fault lines of my heart. & Your mercy floods the spaces in between. I am reborn illuminated & strong, steady as an ice-laden oak against the northern winds. You are a bright moment worth waiting for, & in the circle of Your arms, where our hearts move quietly, I find hope in the silence & despair & Your mercy. I have counted my failures again & again & I will let go. I will not be haunted again.

Aching with Thirst

Psalm 42

Sometimes I nestle my spirit in the rippling creek, aching with a thirst I cannot name. I have always done this, let my spirit rest within some other element that is not myself. I exhale into the rock, the ridges, the river, as easy as a breath into the winds of early summer, & there I lie down gently & become these other things; things that are not fear or doubt or a racing heart. No, I am a fawn that knows only the fresh scent of grass & the ever-rising sun. You settle between my ribs, the rock, the ridges, the river. & when I am beat, down, hurt, or scared, I look up to the hills & You touch me. You are sitting alone by the tallest trees of the valley, perched quietly on a stone, the wild river's roar filling the air. Your hands are clasped in front of You, & all around Your quiet form, the hills rise like citadels & their slopes like sentinels watching us. *Reach for me.* You shift Your weight & turn to face the space where I stand. You lift your hand to gently place my hair behind my ear. The light filtering through the leaves is brighter than before. I focus on the sky. See how the darkest water parts & how I love you like a fire burning in the fragile spaces between the roughened cliffs. I will always turn to You, will always live breathless & free in the breaking. & there is peace by this river, still. All temporal things slip away. Let me not miss this moment; let me strip the blankets of summer & feel the sting of truth, a biting wind along my skin—it sings, & I need You. Don't let me close my eyes, & if I should, let it only be in the circle of Your arms where my heart moves in a quiet beating & the rest is silence & peace. The river of my heart runs

with good water, the sun glinting off the surface each morning &
there is solace in the shining, & I'm a bird singing into the dying of
the day, bravely turning to face the driving wind, wings extended
out & in in the torrents of replenishing rain, bright wings fluttering
in the deepest of deep, but You take my hand in Yours & tell me
even though the sky is falling, there is hope.

Salt & Light

Matthew 5:13–16

The sun shines bright against the clear blue sky. I lift my eyes & my face stretches into a smile. The water rushes up & down over my feet, the smell of salt washing the air, calming me, holding me the way You do. It holds my hands inside its palms, nestles in my windswept hair. A man of the sea, You love the smell of the ocean; You wrap an arm around my shoulder, give me the words for this feeling, this smell of salt an ever-guiding light. The salt is beautiful, crystallized spice & flavor & glint piercing my eyes, a small fragment—vast & wide & full—speaking to me of life, of sins absolved—of wounds, slabs of meat. I rise from it, the sun high above me, its glow falling off my shoulders. I am a little ember glowing as You carry me, Your shadow a halo surrounding my body. We are two bodies, whole. We walk into the water, in silence, inside a fire that draws us close as You whisper my name. The light shines through me. I am a lone lamp standing on its shadow, & as I shine for everyone to see, the wind speaks to me inside this home, a quiet world planning a different tomorrow, a warm place to rest, a clean, well-lighted space. & when You lay me down, I kneel in the sand & hear You speak. Your voice tastes of the ocean I have been craving for so long.

Love Is Greater Than Fear

Luke 12:32–34

When darkness falls gently across these open plains of windswept grass on a hill, it takes nothing but a single breath to lay my spirit bare, fingers of the starlit night reaching into the wild tangles of my hair & how easily I let these barriers fall down, releasing my fear, all the weight I've carried upon my shoulders dropped & how I crumble & fold because I am not afraid to love You. I turn toward the sunlit warmth of Your love, arms reaching out forever; I let them fall, live breathless & free in the breaking knowing I am safe here. & in Your eyes I find myself unafraid, & I extend my hands into the darkness, fingertips aching to lift my spirit, now formed of mountain storms & raging light.

Trust in God

Psalm 56

The wilderness has excavated me, this hard-edged rain thrown from a raging sky, cutting quickly across the exposed contours of my neck. The distant crack of thunder shakes the ground, vibrates along my spine. It does not rumble like a gentle summer storm; it implodes, draws nearer, like the frontlines of a war somewhere in the night. But, I am not afraid. I face the driving wind, arms extended out & in within the torrent of rain, for You are there with me. Your bright wings flutter in the deepest hollows of my despair, their brightness lighting the air between the clashing clouds. & when the lightning flares, I can see You suspended in the air, still. I reach for You & am not afraid. I am a tiger & a fawn, the she-wolf that screams to the moon at dust; the meadowlark that whistles to the sun at dawn. I am the darkness & the light because I trust in You. You protect me, carve out my song & set aside a space where the world's cruelty cannot hurt me. I am safe, heart beating wildly, unafraid of the violence of this wild space, high in these cliffs, delivered.

Only Say the Word

Matthew 8:5–13

The weight I carry pulls me down on this bed. I am holding myself together by the skin of my teeth, laying with these frozen limbs, trying so hard to breathe, to live in a body that is inevitably dying. & I can feel it in my bones, the faintest whisper calling me home. I pray from my naked heart so that, even now, sacred things cling tightly to me, no solace in this suffering until You. *Lord, I am not worthy to receive you.* My bones are laced with silent grief & You kneel beside me, cupping my face in Your hands, reaching through the impenetrable emptiness. *But, only say the word.* I see it in Your eyes, the lingering love, stronger than all the love of man—devoid of fear, unfaltering, pure—so beautiful that when I look at You, I don't want to lose the light. You seek the broken, hold the strays, caress the wounded spaces, trying so hard to mend the pieces, congeal blood from a place of honesty. & now, You, You burn with light. & I can feel sacred things move between us, & all the wounds I have unfurled across my body heal in this cleansing—I am worthy.

Lazarus

John 11:38–43

That night blew darkness into me but You, You whispered my name, splintered apart these eyelids, let the syllables wrap themselves around me, carried me back to you. *Awaken* You said, & so I did & You let the words *Come here* drip into my ears, & so I did. I came back to you, uncurled my body to the sunlight peering itself from behind you & I knelt, knelt for Your touch, knelt for Your words to awaken more than just this, this limp body, give me a reason for being, & so you did, you took this skin & struck life through it, taught me to roll my tongue, to own Your language, & You pressed Your forefinger to my forehead and said *I will take you home.*

& He Wept

John 11:35

Grief walks on blistered feet, hand-in-hand with me through many war-torn streets, kicking up dirt, & my fingers trace the dust of the failures I'm not ashamed of when the nights are so blue & the indigos sink deeper into me, their growth bruising every rib, every gap in my bones leaving an echo etched in fire & I burn like the seasons. But, when it is quiet, Your words awaken me—feather-soft sentences ensconcing my body & setting me free. I've seen You in my smile, shaped just like everything else when I find peace & take root within myself & You weep on the ruins of my spring.

& I Am Stilled

John 11:25–26

See how the gift of this moment recognizes the sharpness of its disappearance, the harshness of its void, & all the deadness I savor in the blackness of the night disappears. Let me hold it as I call out to a silent grave. & when You ask me to rise, lift against the sky, into the stillness of an unsung song, & as my skin splits, my bones drag through the veins of the earth & I rise & set in You, Your word brightens the sky beyond the shadow of my body, & You, in turn, rise inside me until I hear myself sing & am stilled.

Even if Grief Buries My Face

Psalm 31:9–16

I am standing on a narrow ridge, listening for You in a bush burning in the wind, & I can feel you rising, hear myself crying out, a ghostly sobbing, falling on my knees when I call to You. & when I kneel & I hear You speak, Your voice breaks through the deafness drowns out the static of sadness. & I curl up inside Your steadfast love, our bodies nestled together here in this gently drifting dark & unable to feel where my breath ends & Yours begins. I give You my brokenness, rest in Your grace. Even if grief buries my face, even if I feel a dark night spreading inside me, the stars scattered drifts of snow spilled in the wind & crunching under my feet, feel the cold set deep in my bones, a stone-cold desert of bone & ash, the pieces of me irrevocably torn, I will travel over the hunch of the earth seeking Your comfort. & if I should fade again into the cusp of the world, I will return to winter knowing the warmth of the sun at its peak in a vast blue sky, stronger. & the fruiting fig tree will perpetually offer figs; the vine growing grapes that smell like wine; the rivers of living water flowing infinitely. Whether in sorrow or joy, I will serve You. You are the light through the fog & I rise lighter because of it. & I will pray through the hot summer of my faith, & I will walk in Your white footsteps across water, homeward.

Wait for the Lord

Psalm 27

The sky is my silent witness, a cloud-lit space where there is no void, no darkness but meaning in the middle of emptiness, in the dawn waiting at the edge of every midnight. & there's a light that shines in the darkness, a star guiding the way, a gate open, a shepherd waiting to save me. My failures are as beautiful as my triumphs, & my heart beats without knowing its beating. Fishes flow & forests walk & figs grow upon thorn & I seek. I burrow into Your palm & You receive me. & in You, I see the North Star, the tiny green buds of palm trees, a sanctuary in the tiny corner of myself, a refuge that loves me with stretched & open arms. You listen to me & I wait.

His Steadfast Love

Psalm 118

I cannot define this endurance, cannot enter a silence where suffering hangs heavy, suspended in the resonance of the steadfast love that carries & lifts me. Heal me & forgive me in my blindness & I will give thanks. Take my hand & show me a sunlit road where I am found. The water knows the rushing between the rocks, between the wild, green cliffs where a little bird flits & perches on a thorn bush beside the shoreline. I am burning in the bush's fire, churning in waves of the charged ions lifting in monumental drifts from the sun's surface—solar winds I turn my face into & tremble beneath Your salvation, my heart thundering like a colt born of fire, hooves drumming across the curves of your shoulder where I lay my head & how I can never lay close enough in this moment that is no more or less than love. & how it spills like water over rocks. There is beauty here. There is a kingdom of love in Your eyes, inside the voice of the water. & when the sunrise alights the bodies of the palm trees against the sky, when your fingertips brush my tears, there is something holy here, & I should drop to my knees in praise.

Make Me Your Colt

Matthew 21:1–11

You untied my ropes & drew near & I bowed my back to you, baring Your burden. Together we walked over palm fronds spread out by the people & breathed in a thousand *Hossanas.* You come to the gate of my heart, & I raise my hands & sing against the palms piercing at the firmament, piercing the sky, the fronds like feathers, works of art, of the Father, meant to draw You into me, to worry less, to praise more. & You rise in their flutter, the fronds soaring & flapping & shuddering, as if they could fly without hands waiving them, risen off the ground, wandering through the skies. & when the wind died down, the fronds subsided with grace & poise, fresh green covering the sun—swaying, carefree, all eyes on You. & You took to the city, & You took on the city. Untie & set me free again & again, break me. There is such a thing as holy ground & I belong here.

I Carry the Alabaster Jar of My Life into Each New Day

John 12:1–11

The candles stir with soft breath & stir flame within me. Beauty rests in the quietness of this moment, a jar broken open at the intersection of yearning & mourning, of love & loss. & I kneel at Your feet pouring out perfume, the ointment thick in the air, scandalously anointing your aching feet. Let me unbind my hair & let it flow like water over them. Let me wipe them dry with tender & reckless thanksgiving until sweetness fills the room, the house, the night & more people pour to You—You who comes to us in our weeping breaking bread, bringing joy. Beloved, I pour myself out for You, a gesture of absolute giving. Feel me. Let me pour myself out lavishly for You alone, anointing you as you have me, letting the fragrance spread through this ordinary house until I no longer know what calculation & proportion are—until I only know everything—& I give it to you.

The Messenger

Isaiah 50:4–9

You have given me the voice of a teacher, the calm of a mother, &
the warmth of a pastor so that I may extend a cup of cool water
to the thirsty, air to the anxious, word to the weary. You turn me
toward You to listen, open my ears, widen my eyes. I am torn
open, pain ripping across the wound, & I will not turn away or be
terrified. I will offer myself again & again, steadfast in my calling. I
am exposed & do not hide for You are with me inside this vessel, &
I am whole & found in shadow. You stand with me in my suffering,
& I will cling to the promise of a better day.

Wait With Me

Matthew 26:36–46

Gethsemane never sleeps—its gates crack open & the flowers & their brazen roots recall the night they were fed droplets of blood dripping softly on a hallowed ground of lament. *Wait with me.* & I wait with the stars & the wind is still & wide awake. The dead weight of the engulfing darkness presses on, & the olive trees grow east, the bright bare load pushing down on them insisting they spread & bow & pleat back on themselves, crack & hunch—light dropping through the fruit leveling the ground. & as the light falls & flattens what grows in the garden, Your grieved voice speaks into the trees' clefts & curled up, I am awakened by the hot, stilled air. When morning rises slowly & yet still without abating, when it swallows the sun & man, I come to this dark place & look at what can be known in Your breathe & work. & I learn from You, gather grace, understand what death will ask of You—You, man made perfect in God sweating blood: Gethsemane, under your mount of olives, the green-pitted translucence of night, where You writhed at the break of night into the morning blossoms, the red snow of skin shedding against the smell of honeysuckle & hay of manger & His Word becoming flesh—pain opening in this lost garden. Pinned by the weight of my sins, You walked all night alone & wept. *I wait* & I drink the cup of Your pain by Your side, touch the ground in prayer, walk with You in suffering. *I'm awake.*

Lift Your Heel Against Me

John 13:1–20; Luke 22:47–53

The moment I knelt before you, took off your sandals & readied the water, I felt the silver in your pocket slapping your thigh like knives, knowing you want kiss me, & in that kiss, betrayal. I looked up, searched your eyes, & found love, welcomed the kiss, wanting to hear its click on my lips. & as I gently washed your feet, holding each in my hand watching the dirt pool away, feeling bone through hard skin, I knew you would leave me & slip out into the dark night. & before you even reached out your hand, before they counted coins into your palm, I forgave you, handing over the kingdom as small as a mustard seed, as yeast, a box of treasure hidden away beneath the dirt. This is the way there, & when the silence ebbed between us, I gave myself to this inevitable. May you welcome this as what it is, a needful offering that has let go of everything to lay itself at your feet, & I tell you I see you, I bless you, & in this blessing that drenches both the giver & the receiver, there is nothing fuller than this moment.

What Great Love Is This?

John 3:16

I stand in the shadow of the cross where strange birds gather & cry & the afternoon sun vanishes & the fog dims. Father, forgive me, I do not know what I do. I am undone, walking in the darkness, eyes closed, & lash by lash You climb the hill, the pain You bear flowing forgiveness, spreading & transforming, blood mixed with grace & hope watering dry ground, lifting my burdens & carrying them away. In this moment, I hold onto Your words, capture my beginning, again & again. I bear Your pain, watching you twist on those wooden beams, nails piercing You, me, my pain & loss, my heart broken open, scattered, lying in the dirt, for this one last act of love, this giving from an empty cup. & I hold you in my pain, in my sorrow as darkness fills the sky, Your skin filling with fresh bruises, Your eyes painted with tremor, a diadem of sharp pike, its needles pressed into Your brow digging in, wrapping Your head, crowning a body of torn & peeling of skin. I feel your isolation, this darkness without light, & yet within the darkness, I feel You beside me, giving me the courage to cry out of the darkness You have saved me from, again & again. I too am thirsty & You are my source, the spring of my rivers. Grant me grace & let me see You in every thirsty mouth. You carry my sorrow, head bowed, sinking into the final pain of nails, Your body bearing no more having borne it all. Your work is done in the deep darkness over the face of the deep, & the temple torn in two divides God & man—the Father inside Your dying holds You inside His hands, a reconciliation & trust even in the moment of Your last breath teaching me how to die, how to live, take comfort in my end, take comfort in those hands.

55

Speak to Me of Love

John 13:31–35

God is in my heart, & I am the heart of God, His love directing my course with no other desire but to fulfill itself inside me. I will melt into its river & sing its melody to the night, know the pain that comes with its tenderness; suffer & bleed willingly & joyfully when it beckons. I will follow it through its hard & steep ways, yield inside its wings though its pinions may wound me. I will listen to it speak as it grows & prunes me, descends to my roots & shakes them from their clinging to the earth. We are born to love one another—let love be a moving sea between the shores of our spirits. That we should fill our cups but not drink alone, give each other sustenance, become the bread of God's sacred feast, become the lone strings of a violin that quiver together making the same music, just as the oak & cypress cannot grow in each other's shadow. Love so you may know the secrets of your heart. Sleep with a prayer for each other & a song of praise on your lips. Wake at dawn with peace & give thanks for another day of loving.

He Is Risen

Matthew 27:57–66

Behold the spirit bringing you back to life; the promise of an empty tomb driving nails into the darkness. You come forth from the grave as if leaving home—linen left neatly inside, an opened & bare tomb of reconciliation, a thrust-back stone unable to contain what the cross did not destroy. May the sight of You burn me with the flame of grace as I stand beside you awake, arisen with joy. That I am made like You & like You I rise, mine the cross, the grave, the blue voice of skies soft as the gray mist gathering & clinging to You risen in the garden, standing beside Mary, ever new shepherd speaking my name, meeting me in my journey. & I give myself to You, sew in tears with hope to reap joy. I have seen death; I have seen resurrection & keep nothing back. I look for you & find You, & in you, everything.